FOR POLLY – M. C.

AUSTRALIAN MAMMALS

Artwork by
MATT CHUN

LITTLE HARE
www.littleharebooks.com

BRUSH-TAILED ROCK-WALLABY

Brush-tailed rock-wallabies usually live in steep, rocky areas, including cliffs, gorges and rocky outcrops. They are very agile, and their feet have tough, textured padding that protects them from sharp surfaces. They can leap and bound very quickly, even across uneven ground. Their long tails, which have a brush of bushy fur at the end, help keep them balanced. They can also climb trees, using their sharp claws to grip the bark. They were once more widespread, but these wallabies are now mostly concentrated in New South Wales.

Brush-tailed rock-wallabies have large home ranges, usually with one particular area where they sleep. This can be a cave, a crevice, an overhanging rock or any other rocky shelter. These wallabies are quite social and can live in small groups, but generally each have their own den.

Brush-tailed rock-wallabies have compact bodies and shaggy fur in shades of dark brown, grey and rust, sometimes with a burst of white on their chests. Their fur is paler on their bellies and darker on their paws and tails, and they have pale stripes on their cheeks and a dark stripe down the middle of their heads.

Mothers generally raise one baby at a time. The newborn wallabies live in their mother's pouch for a number of months, drinking milk and growing stronger.

Brush-tailed rock-wallabies like to sun themselves regularly, but avoid the heat in the middle of the day. They are generally more active in the evening or the early morning, and often forage for food around dusk. They mostly eat grasses, along with some seeds, fruit, leaves and flowers.

SPOTTED-TAIL QUOLL
(AKA TIGER QUOLL)

Spotted-tail quolls have thick fur in shades of brown and red, with pale bellies and spots of white across their backs and tails. These spots help them blend in to the dappled light of their surroundings. Spotted-tail quolls, also known as tiger quolls, live in forested areas and heaths in certain parts of eastern Australia, particularly Tasmania. Their range used to be much bigger, but it has declined due to loss of habitat and danger from predators.

These quolls are most active at night. During the day, they shelter in their dens, which can be made in rock crevices, caves or hollow logs. Spotted-tail quolls are quite solitary, and have large home ranges that they patrol as they look for food. They are fast and agile, and are even able to climb trees.

Spotted-tail quolls are skilled hunters, with strong jaws and sharp teeth. Their prey includes gliders, possums, rats, bandicoots, rabbits, small wallabies, birds and reptiles, but they can also eat larger animals.

Baby spotted-tail quolls are very small at birth, and continue to develop inside their mother's pouch until they're big enough to be left in the den while she goes out to hunt.

Spotted-tail quolls have quite distinctive calls – particularly the males. They make deep growling sounds and loud spitting noises, and they can also hiss or scream.

_____

GREY-HEADED FLYING FOX

Grey-headed flying foxes are one of the largest bats in Australia. They have soft fur across their bodies and broad, leathery wings. The fur on their heads is grey, and there are shades of brown and dark grey on their bodies. They also have a circle of brighter russet or orange fur around their necks. Unlike other flying foxes, they have fur right down to their ankles.

These flying foxes like to make their homes in forests with thick, dense canopies, where they hang upside down from the trees, but they can also be found in gardens and backyards in more urban areas. They often live in large camps, sometimes made up of tens of thousands of flying foxes, and can stay in one home area for their whole lives.

Grey-headed flying foxes generally forage during the night, and they will travel long distances to find food. They are often called fruit bats, but they eat more pollen and nectar than fruit. They eat from a wide variety of different plants, and often help plants to grow by spreading pollen and nectar between them.

When they're first born, grey-headed flying foxes are carried by their mothers. The babies cling tightly to their mother's fur, and are fed with milk. When they become too big to carry, the babies are left at home in groups while some mothers go out to find food. After a few months, young flying foxes are able to fly, and they become independent not long after.

DINGO

Dingoes are a type of wild dog. They have a naturally lean build, with broad heads, large, pointed ears and bushy tails. Their fur can vary in colour from sandy yellow to a rusty ginger, and is paler on their feet, bellies and the tips of their tails. Dingoes live across Australia in grasslands and deserts, but can also be found in forests and even snowy alpine areas. Dingoes in these places are usually darker brown or tan.

Dingoes are skilled hunters, and only eat meat. They often hunt between dusk and dawn, and sometimes form packs as they search for food. They move swiftly, and can cover a lot of ground. They eat animals such as rabbits, wallabies, kangaroos, rodents and wombats, and sometimes their prey can also include birds, reptiles and insects.

Dingoes mark their home territories with their scent. They also howl to communicate, and very occasionally bark. Home territories can be shared by a group, but dingoes are often solitary. They make dens in caves, rocky shelters or hollow logs, and sometimes even in the old burrow or warren of another animal. Dingoes usually have a few pups at a time, and both parents help to raise them. They live in the den and are fed with milk until they're old enough to start eating solid food, and eventually hunt for themselves.

KOALA

Koalas have stocky bodies and thick, soft fur. Their fur can range from ash-grey to brown, with a creamy colour on their chests and bellies. Their large, black noses are hairless.

Koalas generally live in the east of Australia, and they spend most of their time in eucalyptus forests. They can venture down to the ground, but they prefer to be up in the trees. Their strong arms, flexible fingers and sharp claws help them grip onto branches, making them excellent climbers.

Koalas can sleep for up to eighteen hours each day, perched comfortably in the forks of trees. They often snooze through the day and wake up at night. Although they can be sleepy and quiet, koalas are able to move very quickly, especially along the ground, and they also make loud growling, grunting or bellowing sounds.

Baby koalas are very small when they're born, so they stay inside their mother's pouch and drink milk until they grow bigger. Even after leaving the pouch, a young koala will stay close to its mother, often clinging to her tummy or back.

Koalas sometimes eat flowers, stems, fruit and bark, but they mostly eat eucalyptus leaves. These leaves are poisonous to many other animals, but koalas can break them down and get their nutrients without being harmed. They can eat over one kilogram of leaves in a single day.

QUOKKA

Quokkas are a particularly small type of wallaby – the smallest in Australia. Their grey-brown fur is darker on top of their bodies and paler underneath, and it is very thick. Their broad faces have bare black noses and mouths that often look as if they're smiling.

Quokkas live in the south-west of Western Australia, both on the mainland and on two islands off the coast, Rottnest Island and Bald Island. They live in a variety of habitats, including heaths and shrubland. They often live near streams or swamps, but can also live in drier areas. They prefer a warm climate, but can handle cooler temperatures.

Quokkas generally take shelter during the day in areas of dense vegetation, which they burrow into. They make little tunnels through the plants so that they can move around easily while still staying under cover.

When they move, quokkas either hop or walk along the ground with a bounding gait. They can also climb trees, which they generally do to find food.

Quokkas only eat plants, and often forage for food in groups. They like to eat grasses and leaves, especially tender new growth, and sometimes eat bark or stems. They usually rest during the day and forage for food at night, although quokkas on Rottnest Island have adjusted to be more active during the day.

Quokkas have one baby at a time, and it lives in its mother's pouch and drinks milk until it is big enough to find its own food.

———————————

RED KANGAROO

Red kangaroos are tall and muscular, with dense, velvety fur across their bodies. Males are red or orange, while females are grey-blue. Both males and females have paler fur on their chests and bellies, as well as black and white patches on their cheeks and a white stripe stretching from their mouths to their large, softly pointed ears.

Red kangaroos use their powerful hind legs to hop, and their long tails to keep them balanced. They can move very swiftly, and jump to extraordinary heights. Females are often smaller, and they're faster, too.

Red kangaroos live in groups, also called mobs, in open plains and sparsely wooded areas across Australia. The members of the group look out for each other. They often live in places that are quite dry and warm, and they like to lounge in shady areas during the heat of the day.

When they're first born, red kangaroo joeys are only as big as a jellybean. They have to stay tucked away in a pouch on the front of their mother's body until they get bigger. Even after they're big enough to venture out, joeys still hop back into their cosy pouch from time to time.

Young red kangaroos drink their mother's milk, but as they get older, they start to eat things like grasses and leaves. Red kangaroos don't need to drink much water, as the plants they eat have liquid in them.

COMMON BRUSH-TAILED POSSUM

Common brush-tailed possums have thick, soft fur in shades of silvery grey and coppery brown. Their fur is paler on their bellies and darker towards the end of their long, bushy tails. They often have a dark band of fur across their snouts or between their eyes, and their large, gently pointed ears are tipped with white.

Common brush-tailed possums live in many parts of Australia, and are particularly widespread along the east coast. They live in forests and wooded areas, and spend most of their time in trees. They are excellent at climbing, with sharp claws to grip bark and the ability to leap between branches. They often curl up in tree hollows to sleep, but they can also make cosy homes in logs, piles of rocks and other sheltered areas. If they have trouble finding places to live in their natural habitat, they can move into urban areas and make their homes there.

One baby brush-tailed possum is usually born at a time, and it lives inside its mother's pouch and drinks milk as it continues to grow. After leaving the pouch, a young possum stays with its mother, often riding on her back, until it's fully independent.

Common brush-tailed possums generally rest during the day and forage for food at night. They eat leaves, buds, fruit and blossoms from a range of plants, and sometimes they also eat insects and bird eggs. In urban areas, they eat an even broader range of things.

These possums can be quite vocal, with a wide range of sounds that include screeches, growls, screams, grunts, hisses, coughs and clicks.

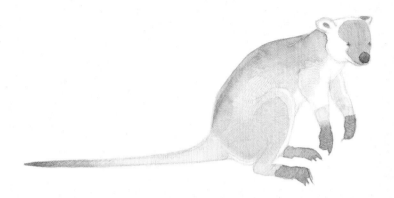

LUMHOLTZ'S TREE KANGAROO

Lumholtz's tree kangaroos live in Queensland. They live in forests, particularly rainforests, and often high in the canopy where they are hidden among the foliage. They mostly eat leaves, along with certain flowers and fruit. Some of the leaves they eat are toxic to most other mammals, but these tree kangaroos are able to digest them.

Lumholtz's tree kangaroos are active at night and sleep during the day. They have a spiral shape in their fur that helps rain to flow more easily off their bodies when they're curled up in the fork of a tree.

They have thick, dark fur across their bodies, with paler fur on their lower backs and a band of pale fur running across their foreheads and down each side of their faces. Their front arms are strong and good for climbing, with long claws and pads of skin to help grip onto branches. Their back legs are shorter and broader, but still with a soft pad underneath.

Their thick tails are tipped with black fur, and can be longer than their entire bodies. Their tails aren't flexible enough to wrap around branches, but they do help the animals to keep their balance when climbing through the trees. On the ground, or along large, flat branches, Lumholtz's tree kangaroos move by hopping. They can also leap enormous distances between branches.

Lumholtz's tree kangaroos only have one baby at a time, and they don't have one every year. It takes a long time for their babies to grow inside the womb, and baby tree kangaroos stay inside their mother's pouch for many months, too.

COMMON WOMBAT

Common wombats are compact and stocky, with broad shoulders, blocky heads and short, strong legs. Their thick, coarse fur can vary in colour from dark brown to grey or paler, sandy shades. Their tail is very small and tucks in neatly at the back of their bodies. They are one of the largest burrowing animals in the world, with tough, flattened claws that are well-suited to digging.

These wombats are mainly found in south-eastern Australia. They spend much of their lives inside their burrows, which are often large, complex structures with many different tunnels and rooms. They prefer to live in forests and wooded areas, and often dig into sloped areas to make their homes.

Common wombats are generally solitary, although their home ranges can overlap. When threatened, wombats can use their strong backsides to block the entrance to their burrow. They can also move incredibly quickly.

Baby wombats are very small when they're born, so they climb inside a pouch on their mother's body to keep developing for many months. After leaving the pouch, they stay with their mothers for a while longer. Mothers and babies speak to each other with soft 'huh' sounds, but common wombats can also growl and hiss to express alarm or make threats, including to other wombats.

Common wombats generally hide out in their burrows throughout the hottest parts of the day and come out after sunset to forage. They sometimes eat bark, dry leaves, stalks and roots, but they mainly use their sharp incisor teeth to feed on grass. They are particularly fond of native grasses such as kangaroo grass, tussock grass and wallaby grass.

GREATER BILBY

Greater bilbies live in places that are hot and dry, including deserts, grasslands and plains. They were once quite widespread, but are now only found in a handful of places. They're burrowing animals, and spend their days tucked away underground, safe from heat and predators. Their burrows are long, with a twisting, spiralling shape, and they often use the same burrow for many years.

Greater bilbies' small bodies are covered in long, silky fur, which is blue-grey on top and tan or cream underneath. Their thin tails have distinctive bands of black-and-white fur at the ends. These bilbies use their hind legs to hop, and their smaller front arms, tipped with sharp claws, are used for digging.

Babies are often born in pairs, and mothers can raise young multiple times in a year. The tiny newborns are kept in their mother's pouch at first, where they drink milk. After venturing out of the pouch, young bilbies stay in the burrow. Their mother brings food back to them until the young bilbies are ready to set out on their own.

Greater bilbies eat both plants and animals, and they usually leave their burrows at night to look for food. Despite their large eyes, they don't have particularly good eyesight, so they use their keen sense of smell and their large, delicate ears to find food. They often use their long, sticky tongues to lick up insects and their larvae, especially termites, but they also eat seeds, fruit and bulbs, as well as lizards and other small animals. They don't need a lot of water, as they get some liquid from the food they eat.

FEATHERTAIL GLIDER

Feathertail gliders are the smallest gliding mammals in the world. Their tiny bodies can fit in the palm of your hand, and are covered with short, silky fur. Most of their fur is a grey-brown, but their underbellies are a soft, pale cream.

These gliders live in forests and wooded areas in eastern Australia. They occasionally go down to the ground, but they spend most of their lives high in the treetops. Their feet have large, serrated pads that help them grip onto branches, even when the bark is very smooth.

Feathertail gliders can leap extraordinary distances between trees. Their front and back limbs are joined by a layer of very thin skin, which catches the air when the gliders stretch out their limbs and leap. Their tails are flattened and have a fringe of long, stiff hairs on either side – almost like a feather. The gliders use their tails to steer as they soar between trees.

Feathertail gliders make their tiny, spherical nests in tree hollows, lining them with leaves and bark. Sometimes, they use nests built by birds. These gliders live in groups, and sometimes multiple females share a nest during breeding season. Feathertail gliders usually have two to four babies at a time, and each one is smaller than a grain of rice. These tiny newborns are kept in their mother's pouch until they've grown big enough to live outside. Young feathertail gliders drink milk, then move on to pollen and nectar, as well as some insects. Their long, thin tongues have a special brush at the tip that helps them to pick up the pollen and nectar from blossoms.

SHORT-BEAKED ECHIDNA

Short-beaked echidnas live in a wide range of habitats, including forests and grasslands. They wander long distances through their home ranges in search of food, moving with a slow, rolling gait.

They have small, rounded bodies, which are covered with a layer of dark hair. The sharp spines across their backs are used for protection – when they're threatened, echidnas curl up so that just their spiny outers are visible.

Short-beaked echidnas often have just one baby at a time. Females lay small, leathery eggs, which are kept inside a pouch on the underside of the mother's body. When they hatch, baby echidnas – also called puggles – are very little. They stay inside the pouch and continue to grow, drinking their mother's milk, but leave as their small spines start to become prickly.

Short-beaked echidnas have slender beaks and long, sticky tongues. They are excellent at sniffing out insects, and are particularly fond of ants and termites. They use their sharp claws to break into their nests, then lick up the insects inside.

When it is hot, short-beaked echidnas rest during the middle of the day, becoming more active in the early morning or after dusk. When resting, they often tuck themselves inside logs or rocky crevices. They can also burrow under leaves or even into the soil – their short, claw-tipped feet are perfect for digging. Short-beaked echidnas can also swim, poking their beaks out of the water so they can breathe as they paddle.

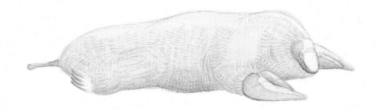

SOUTHERN MARSUPIAL MOLE

Southern marsupial moles are small enough to curl into the palm of your hand. Their bodies are covered in smooth, glossy cream-and-gold fur. They live in the hot, sandy deserts of central Australia, and they spend nearly all of their time underground.

These moles tunnel through the ground in almost constant motion, digging away the sand from in front of them and then pushing it back to close up their tunnels behind them. They have wide, flat claws on their front paws, perfect for scooping sand. They also use their snouts, which have a solid pad on the front, to help shift sand. They have no visible eyes or ears on the outside of their bodies, and their body temperature is the same as their sandy surroundings, helping them to conserve energy.

Southern marsupial moles are kept inside their mother's pouch when they are first born, and are fed with milk when they are young. As they grow older, they eat insects, along with insect eggs and larvae.

As they surface so rarely, there is much that is not yet known about southern marsupial moles.

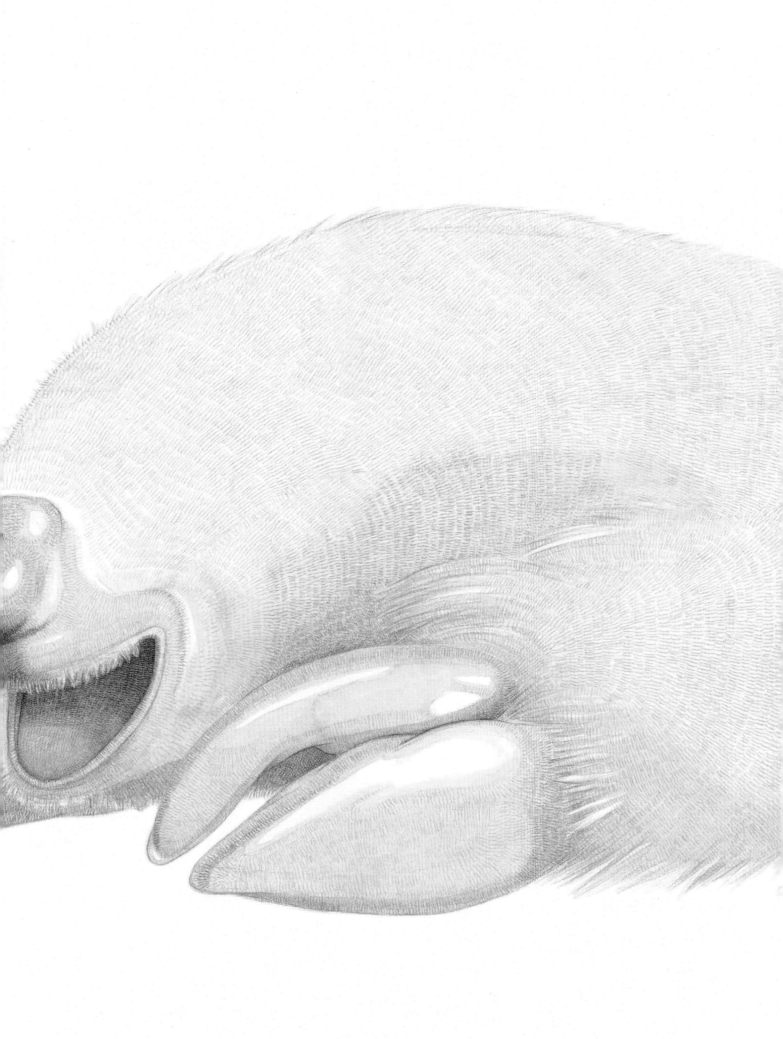

PLATYPUS

Platypuses live on land and in water, but their streamlined bodies are particularly well-suited to swimming. Their fur is dense and waterproof, dark brown on top with a creamy colour underneath. Platypuses close their eyes when they dive, and they also seal their noses and ears. When swimming, they use their tail and back legs to steer, and their front feet to paddle. Their stocky legs are tipped with partially webbed claws, and this webbing can retract on land to make walking easier. Platypuses are fast and graceful in the water, but quite slow and ungainly on land.

Platypuses can be found in freshwater environments in the east of Australia, making their homes in burrows in the banks of rivers, streams, creeks and ponds. Although they can share waterways, they are mostly quite solitary animals.

They emerge from their burrows in the evenings to forage for food, which includes insect larvae, tadpoles, worms, swimming beetles, snails, and water bugs. Platypuses often dive down to the lower parts of the water to find food, picking up loose rocks, dirt and vegetation in their bills and sifting through it to find things to eat. They store any food they find in pouches in their cheeks, then swim to the surface of the water to eat. They have coarse plates inside their bills to grind up their food.

Platypuses usually lay two eggs at a time, which they hold snug against their stomachs with their broad tails. After hatching, the young platypuses stay in the burrow and are fed with milk until they grow big enough to venture outside.

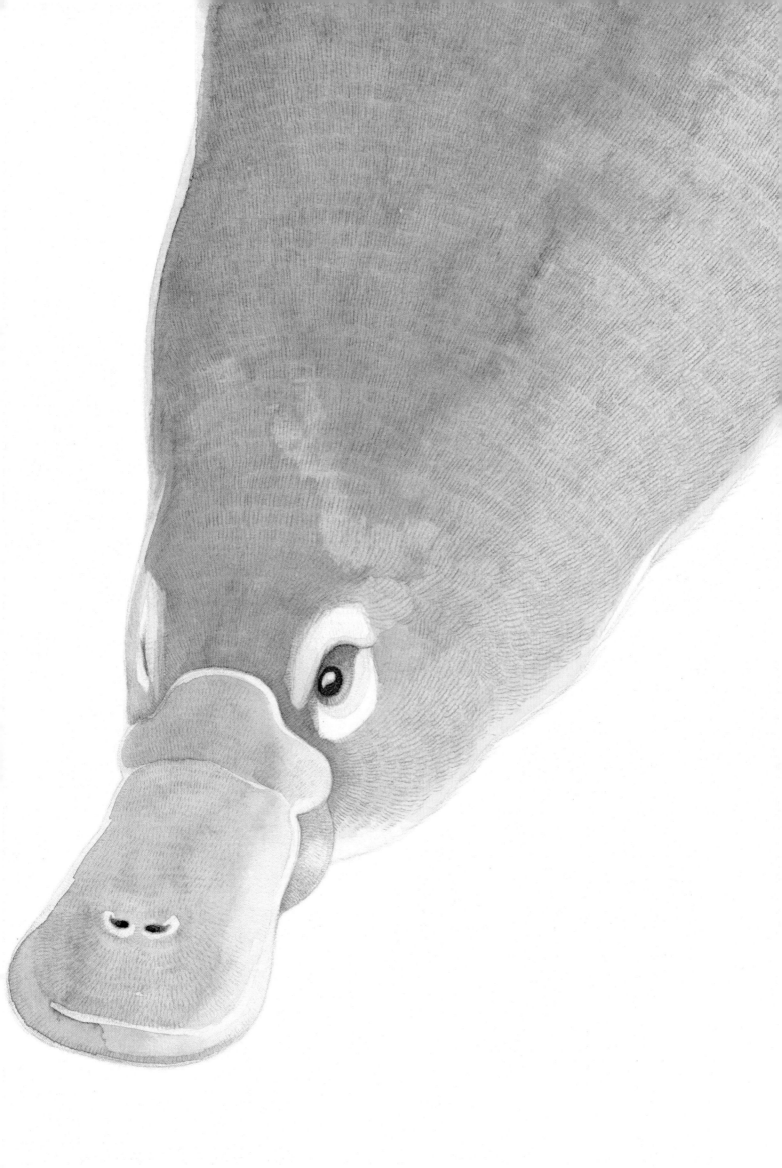

TASMANIAN DEVIL

Tasmanian devils only live in Tasmania. They can live happily in a wide range of habitats, as long as they have enough food and suitable spots to shelter, but they particularly like forests and heaths. They sleep in dens, which are often made in hollow logs or rock crevices. Sometimes they also make use of an old wombat burrow, or sleep in dense parts of the forest under cover of plants.

Tasmanian devils have coarse black fur, with white markings on their chests, flanks and rumps. Their blunt snouts are tipped with long, sensitive whiskers, and their back legs are slightly smaller than those at the front, which gives them an unusual, rolling gait.

Tasmanian devils generally raise two babies, called joeys, at a time. When they're born, the joeys crawl through their mother's fur and into her pouch, where they stay tucked away drinking milk until they're ready to enter the world. Tasmanian devils are very playful when they're young, and like to climb trees and wrestle with each other.

Tasmanian devils hunt at night and sleep during the day. They only eat meat, using their excellent hearing and vision to track down food, which includes small mammals, birds and snakes. They have strong jaws and sharp teeth – for their size, they have one of the most powerful bites of any animal in the world. Despite being skilled hunters, they often eat animals that are already dead, and they eat every part of each animal, including bones and fur. Tasmanian devils often eat in packs. If they want to show their dominance, they open their jaws wide and bare their teeth. They can also make a range of threatening sounds, including loud growling, snarling, coughing, howling and screeching.

Little Hare Books
an imprint of
Hardie Grant Egmont
Ground Floor, Building 1, 658 Church Street
Richmond, Victoria 3121, Australia

www.littleharebooks.com

 A catalogue record for this
book is available from the
National Library of Australia

9781760506759 (hbk.)

Designed by Pooja Desai
Text by Ella Meave
Produced by Pica Digital, Singapore
Printed through Asia Pacific Offset
Printed in Shenzhen, Guangdong Province, China

5 4 3 2 1

Hardie Grant acknowledges the Traditional Owners of the country on which we work,
the Wurundjeri people of the Kulin nation and the Gadigal people of the Eora nation,
and recognises their continuing connection to the land, waters and culture. We pay our
respects to their Elders past, present and emerging.